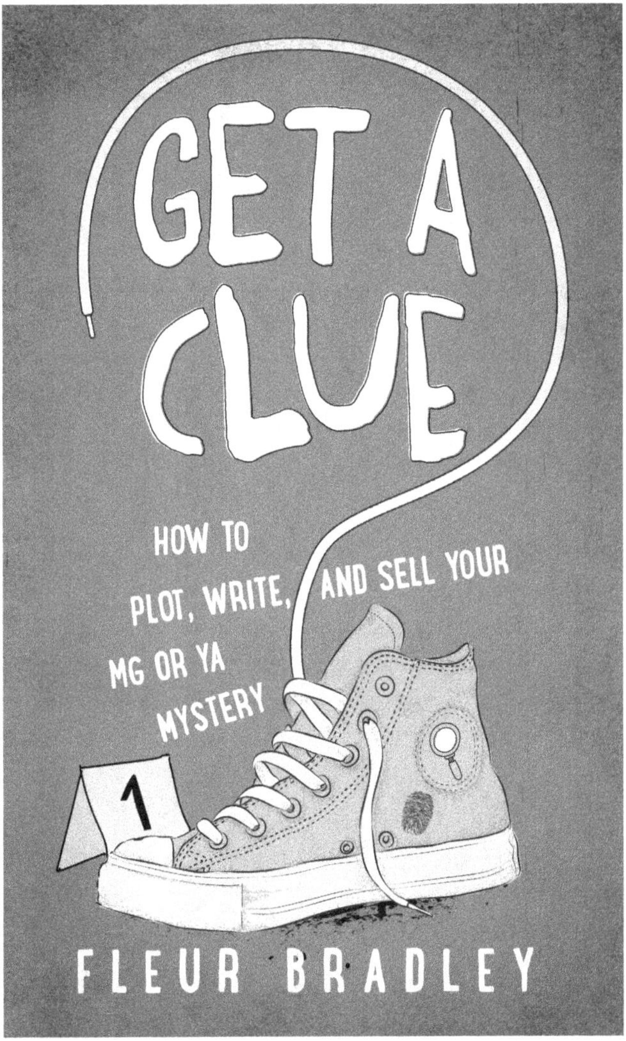
GET A CLUE
HOW TO PLOT, WRITE, AND SELL YOUR MG OR YA MYSTERY
1
FLEUR BRADLEY

Copyright © [2026] by [Fleur Bradley]

All rights reserved. This book or parts thereof may not be reproduced in any form, stored in any retrieval system, or transmitted in any form by any means (electronic, mechanical, photocopy, recording, or otherwise) without prior written permission of the publisher, except as provided by United States of America copyright law and fair use. For permission requests, write to the publisher via the Contact page, www.ftbradley.com.

Library of Congress Control Number: 2026908083

Disclaimer: This book and the content provided herein are for educational purposes and do not take the place of legal advice from your agent or attorney. Effort has been made to ensure that the content provided is accurate and helpful for my readers at publishing time. However, this is not an exhaustive treatment of the subjects. No liability is assumed for losses or damages due to the information provided. You should consult your attorney for your specific publishing and disclaimer questions and needs.

Cover Design by Damonza

ISBN Print: 9798993730707

ISBN ebook: 9798993730714

For information about special discount, bulk sales, or other promotional orders, contact Fleur Bradley at www.fleurbradley.com.

Contents

Introduction	1
1. The Setup	8
2. The Story	16
3. Character	26
4. The Crime	33
The Crime and Place	
Your Turn	
5. Setting and Research	38
6. Finding Time to Write	43
Your Turn	
7. Plotting with Sequences	48
Sequence 1	
Sequence 2	
Sequence 3	
Sequence 4	
Midpoint	

Sequence 5
   Sequence 6
   Sequence 7
   Sequence 8

8. Placing Clues and Red Herrings   91

9. Rough Draft and How to Stay Motivated   97

10. Revision: Where the Real Work Happens   102

11. Marketing & Selling   108

12. School Visits and Speaking   117

13. Final Thoughts and Resources   119

About Fleur Bradley   122

Fleur Bradley's Books   123

Introduction

I '**M FLEUR, AND I love mysteries.**

This is how I open my book talks, whether I'm talking to adults at a literacy event or I'm at a school for an author visit. I love the genre—in fact, I got my start as a writer of short mysteries and crime fiction. For about a decade, short stories were all I wrote.

Eventually, I found my way to the middle-grade novel writing side, still focusing on mysteries. The Double Vision trilogy was my first published set of novels; other works of mine include *Midnight at the Barclay Hotel* and *Daybreak on Raven Island*, as well as numerous non-fiction titles, mostly for the educational market.

My books have won a few awards, including the Colorado Book Award and SCBWI's Crystal Kite Award, and have been nominated for mystery's Anthony and Agatha Awards. A short story of mine, *How to Teach Yourself to Swim*, was chosen for the annual Best Mystery Stories of the Year anthology.

I am the current President of the Rocky Mountain Chapter of Mystery Writers of America. I've judged and chaired the Edgar Awards on the MG and YA side.

I don't share this bio to show off—I just hope it shows that my love for mystery transcends kidlit/MG/YA, and spans a full career.

In short: mysteries are my jam.

I love the puzzle, figuring out whodunit in a game with the author. It makes me feel smart, and every time I read a mystery I learn something new about the craft.

I love the psychology behind crime fiction. Why does someone commit a crime? How can I relate to the antagonist as a reader? Mysteries explore the human psyche in a way no other genre does.

I've blended mysteries with the paranormal (ghosts anyone?), but at their heart my stories are always mysteries.

I hope my enthusiasm for the genre helps you feel that you are in good hands. I want to help you succeed in writing *your* MG or YA mystery.

Why Mysteries for Kids Are Important

I'm not the only reader who's into the genre. Everyone loves a mystery. No, really—or at least a very good number of readers and TV viewers. Mysteries are only second to romance as the most popular fiction genre... With adult readers anyway.

And yet...

The kid mystery department does not reflect this popularity. And we're losing readers by the boatload with each rising grade level.

Fleur pulls out her soapbox.

Take a classroom of third graders. About 89 percent read for fun—not bad, all things considering. Between TV, phones, and other distractions, sometimes I think it's a miracle kids read at all.

Now, let's watch those kids age. If you were to meet that same classroom in eighth grade, reading for fun plummets to 59 percent. And that's the stats (which are somewhat dated anyway) talking—anecdotally, I would say it's much worse.

How do mysteries come into play, you ask?

Mysteries are fun. They're puzzles that appeal to everyone, because we like to feel smart when we solve the thing. Even the most reluctant of readers will be tempted by a good mystery.

I can't back this up with statics, much as I'd like to, but... I believe mysteries can keep kids reading for fun. So, us authors have an important job.

All soapbox stuff aside, if you picked up this book you probably already love mysteries yourself. Writing mysteries for MG or YA readers is so rewarding; I speak from experience.

How Mysteries Are Different

As you go through this book, you'll recognize some of the plotting methods if you're a more experienced writer. The truth is, mysteries for kids are like any other book: you need a solid plot, three-dimensional characters with stakes, and a resolution that makes reading the book fulfilling.

However, mysteries are different in that you need to set up the puzzle, or the game you're about to play with your reader. Although you don't want to resort to stereotypes (more on this later), you do want the clue-type mystery to be a fun one for your reader to solve.

Mystery writers need to plot more carefully. They must reveal clues or red herrings at the right time. A good mystery gets this just right. A bad one is a disappointment.

Not to worry, we'll make sure your mystery is the former.

How Mysteries for Kids Are Different

If you are writing a middle-grade mystery (or a chapter book), you'll want to keep any danger and complexity age-appropriate. The best way to figure out what's okay and what isn't is to imagine telling the story to your target reader. A twelve-year-old will be ready for different content than an eight-year-old, or a middle-schooler reading YA. There are no hard rules when it comes to what's okay and what isn't. It's a judgment call in the end.

Crime and the motivation to commit one can go dark or stay light, like in a cozy mystery. Read widely in the age category you want to write for. You'll get a nose for what's cool and what you should avoid.

Mysteries for YA are less restrictive. You can pretty much go as dark or light as you want with your mystery. Just make sure you understand that this may affect whether a library shelves your book or not.

What This Book Is (and Is Not)

There are a lot (like *a whole lot*) of books out there on the craft of writing. This book is not a deep-dive into character or a waxing-poetic/philosophical look into the life of a creator. There are great books already on the shelf like that. I don't have anything to add.

This book is a practical look at how to plot a mystery for kids and teens.

I'll recap each chapter and give you a to-do list you can follow for the best results in writing your mystery. This book will guide you to get the words on the page, then revise them so they're ready for submission. I'm a pragmatist at the end of the day. I just want to get on with the mystery, and with this book, I want to help you write yours.

If you follow along with this book, you can have a finished novel draft, timeline depending on how fast you write and revise.

Your Turn

Each chapter has a Your Turn section, where you can apply your new knowledge so you can write your own mystery. By the end of the sequence plotting, you'll have an outline, and you can start writing. I'll even walk you through the broad strokes of revision and briefly cover markets to sell your mystery for kids or teens to.

Let's do this thing.

Chapter 1
The Setup

Hatching Your Idea

WHERE DO YOU GET your ideas...? It's a question I get at just about every author school visit, and I love answering it. Because the possibilities are endless when I'm brainstorming.

I pick up ideas *EVERYWHERE*. When I go to a museum, watch a movie, go for a walk, watch true crime, or read a book. Or ask that question: what if...?

The idea stage is the best one, but also the most terrifying. Because you can start a story or full-blown novel and get this part wrong. I have several fifty-page partial manuscripts that simply died out. Sometimes an idea just isn't ready yet. For me, I often need an interesting setting. Or I need to mash several good ideas together to make a novel that is compelling enough to make a well-rounded story.

It's kind of a magic brew. During author visits, I always tell the kids that a book is like a recipe. You can start with, say, a can of beans. But you need other ingredients to decide what the dish you're cooking is going to be.

To get you started on your mystery, let's begin with the good stuff.

The Crime

What's the crime? If you're writing a mystery, you'll have to figure out what that's going to be sooner or later. Whether you start this brainstorming session with the mystery or it's something you add, you'll have to plot this part of your book carefully.

Once upon a time you couldn't have a murder mystery in middle-grade, but that's changed (or *Midnight at the Barclay Hotel* wouldn't be out there in the world). If you're writing for younger readers just make sure you stay on the cozy side of crime: that means no graphic violence.

> **In MG, the focus should be on solving the puzzle and putting the clues together, not the details of the crime.**

If you're writing YA, you can go a little deeper when it comes to the morality questions surrounding the crime. There really are no rules in YA, though it's important to understand that if your book is graphic in violence or other content anywhere, libraries and schools may not want to shelve your book.

And of course, your protagonist and reader won't be able to solve the mystery without clues. We'll delve into how to place clues later. For now, just think about the mystery or crime that you want at the center of your story. I'll cover this in more detail in Chapter 4.

Is Your Story MG or YA?

If you're new to writing for kids and teens, you may have a tough time figuring out if what you're writing is middle-grade (MG) or YA. MG is geared toward readers aged 8-12, and YA is for readers 12 and up. Then there is the chapter book market of course, which covers the Magic Treehouse series and similar, shorter books.

There is no one-size-fits-all answer to whether your book should be a MG or YA. The best way is to look at your character, content and voice. How old is your protagonist? Is the content and voice more kid-appropriate, or are you dealing with teen issues, like sex and the darker elements of crime? For the U.S. publishing market, MG generally has a protagonist aged 11 or 12, YA's protagonists are 16 or 17. This is a generalization, but it gives you an idea of where your book might fit. Reading widely in your intended segment helps; we'll go into finding comparable titles in the next chapter.

Sometimes It Takes Patience

Take *Midnight at the Barclay Hotel,* my middle-grade (that means it's for kids ages 8-12) mystery that has done pretty well. If you looked at my early notes on this idea, I was going in the wrong direction. And I could feel it. I knew I wanted to write a middle-grade mystery, Agatha Christie style. A classic mystery that could serve as an introduction to the genre for kids.

Great concept. I attribute the book's success to that clear vision. But in my early brainstorming sessions, I had the book set at a museum, one like the Denver Museum of Nature and Science. In case you've never been, it's a very cool, huge museum, with different sections for different topics and time periods—like the Smithsonian. I love it. Excellent choice for a setting if I do say so myself.

But it didn't work with my Agatha Christie style concept. I brainstormed and eventually set the idea aside. It just wasn't ready.

Then I went to the Stanley Hotel here in Colorado. You may be familiar with it as the inspiration behind *The Shining* (movie with creepy Jack Nickolson, based on the book by Stephen King). The Stanley Hotel is very atmospheric and even has a ghost hunting tour. The pieces clicked for me then: my Agatha Christie style mystery for kids, complete with over-the-top characters and a bonafide murder mystery, set in a fictional hotel modeled after The Stanley.

I wrote the introduction of the book in one super-inspired sitting. The words in those first five or so pages have changed a tiny bit since that initial draft, but the intro set the tone for the whole book and largely remained the same.

I had my hook. I had my recipe.

Here's an exercise that works well for me as I'm writing:

Start by finding a basket or a box.

The idea is to fill it with ideas and inspiration. You can also use a pinboard or mood board (for you Pinterest or Canva friends), but I'm a tactile person so I use a basket or a box at this stage in the writing process. In case you think I came up with this genius idea, I didn't. I stole it from the brilliant Twyla Tharp who suggested it in her book *The Creative Habit*.

Your job for this part of the process is to fill your basket, box, or mood board with inspiration for your mystery. For as long as you're working on this novel, it will act as a creative safety deposit box of sorts, guarding your idea.

If you get sidetracked, refer to the box. If you're not sure where the next chapter is going, you'll refer to the box. When you lose faith, you'll—

Well, you get the idea. If you have a dedicated writing space, you can obviously put your inspiration all over, and tape it on your walls. But I like the idea of a box (or in my case: a basket) because anyone can make room for that. Even if you don't have a dedicated office space in your home, finding a box is doable.

I encourage you to find somewhere for your ideas to go, too.

Your Turn

Find a box. For the next week, one hour a day, fill it with what inspires your work.

Ideas:

1. **Comparable titles.** Yes, you can dream about being Stephen King or Katherine Applegate here. Just make sure that the books you add as inspiration are ones that fit your concept. Who is going to read your book? Where will it be placed at your favorite bookstore, on a display table...? Find the books that inspired you to want to write. We'll talk more about these comp titles in the next chapter.

2. **Research books and/or notes.** I'm old school and like to use a notebook for each book. I brainstorm, write research notes, etc. all in this one notebook. The beauty? It costs about a buck for a basic

notebook. Less if you buy them during back-to-school season.

You can also add actual reference books as you gather them.

It's easy to find what you need and stay inspired if you have it all in one place.

3. A planning calendar. This is where you'll chart your progress. You can do this on paper (hello, analog friends!) or on your computer.

4. Anything that inspires you to write. A picture of your family, you as a kid, your favorite bookstore and where your book will be shelved, whatever moves you. Writing a book is hard. Let this box (or basket) help you as you write these coming months.

For about a week, one hour a day, allow yourself to just be inspired. You can jot notes in your fresh new notebook.

Chapter 2
The Story

Defining Your Idea and Plot Description

T HIS IS WHERE WE must slow our roll for a moment. Sure, you think you're ready to outline that amazing new mystery opus. You already picture yourself at your local bookstore, signing your name in that famous author-style illegible scribble, and...

We have to write the thing first, and to do that, we need to lay the foundation for your story. This takes some discipline if you have an exciting idea and just want to get writing already, but Future You will thank you. Making sure you create a strong foundation for your story keeps you from stalling out by page fifty or ending up with a junk novel that stays in the drawer.

In journalism, they're the who, what, where, when, why questions. You want to answer them to keep your story's focus.

This is a lot of fun to plot, because anything is possible.

Writing a Book Jacket Description

I'm a sucker for a good movie. And now that I'm a writer, watching movies is a great exercise in recognizing story structure. It's why I plot in sequences.

We'll get to that later though. First, we need a good foundation to build our novel outline on.

Pretend You're a Reader

Or why pretend—if you're like most novelists, you're probably a bigger reader than you are a writer, right? So how do you decide if a novel is for you, as a reader? Of course, you'll look at the cover. But then...

Chances are, you read the jacket copy. Once you find your way past the blurbs, telling you how this book is the best thing since sliced bread, you'll find the book description. And maybe you'll even read the first few pages, if it sounds good.

This week, we're going to write that book jacket copy. It'll become the yellow line on the road during our novel writing journey.

Hunting ghosts and solving the case before checkout? All in a weekend's work.

Read the novel that New York Times best-selling author, Chris Grabenstein calls, "My kind of mystery!"

When JJ Jacobson convinced his mom to accept a surprise invitation to an all-expenses-paid weekend getaway at the illustrious Barclay Hotel, he never imagined that he'd find himself in the midst of a murder mystery. He thought he was in for a run-of-the-mill weekend ghost hunting at the most haunted spot in town, but when he arrives at the Barclay Hotel and his mother is blamed for the hotel owner's death, he realizes his weekend is going to be anything but ordinary.

Now, with the help of his new friends, Penny and Emma, JJ has to track down a killer, clear his mother's name, and maybe even meet a ghost or two along the way.

This is the jacket for my MG mystery *Midnight at the Barclay Hotel*. Juicy, no?

Who's Your Reader? Imagine your reader as they walk into your favorite independent bookstore. Where will they find your book?

When It's Good to Compare Yourself to Others

We all know it's a bad idea to compare ourselves to others. It just makes you feel like garbage, and who wants that? You be you, I say. But. For this exercise, I want you to imagine that big table at the front of the store.

What books does yours sit next to? In publishing, we call those comparables: basically, books that are like yours.

It's how you'll eventually pitch the book to agents, how your agent will pitch the book to editors, and how editors pitch your book to their team, to convince them that you deserve that big fat advance.

I know, we're getting ahead of ourselves a little there. But in this case, you'll want to jump the gun. The easier it is to pitch your book idea, the easier time you'll have making it through the writing and editing, and eventually the publishing journey.

Examples of (very, very) short pitches I use at book signings when I'm talking to adults:

Double Vision: James Bond meets *Diary of a Wimpy Kid*.

Midnight at the Barclay Hotel: Agatha Christie for kids.

Daybreak on Raven Island: Alfred Hitchcock for kids.

There's a trend there... Note that these pitches aren't exact matches for plot, and they're super short. I usually end up explaining the plot, briefly, if I'm telling someone about my books. These pitches just tell you what the reading experience will be.

This is especially important when writing for kids, because you're often persuading parents, teachers and librarians to pick up your book for your readers. These gatekeepers are not going to read it. They just need to know who this book is right for.

Pitch examples for books that are not mine:

A group of toys that come to life grapple with their role as their kid owner ages (*Toy Story*)

A boy in witness protection is torn between staying safe and solving his friend's murder (*Fake ID* by Lamar Giles)

In the tradition of Nancy Drew, four kids and one grandfather in Miami tackle a decades-old mystery. (*The Sherlock Society* by James Ponti)

Three friends who team up to crack the codes and find a hidden treasure in an abandoned 1950's funhouse. (*The Mystery of Locked Rooms* by Lindsay Currie)

> **Tip from Fleur:** publishers have started to list the short book pitch in bold online, before they give you the book jacket description. Check out Bookshop.org and put in your comparable titles to see this in action.

A good short pitch conveys the feeling or experience for the reader. You can use movies or TV shows instead of books, too.

Those examples are very short pitches, and we don't need them to be perfect right now. But you should know what your comparable titles are.

Need more help? Look at the inside jacket of the library edition of a book where all the publisher and copyright info is; it often has a very short pitch, likely for book sellers and librarians so they know where to shelve it. Another good source is Publishers Marketplace and Publishers Weekly; both of these publishing industry publications list the short pitch that sold the book.

We want that for ourselves, right? So let's make sure the concept and pitch are as strong as can be.

This is the deal announcement and pitch used for *Daybreak on Raven Island*. It was announced in Publishers Weekly.

Aneeka Kalia at Viking has acquired *Daybreak on Raven Island* by **Fleur Bradley** (*Midnight at the Barclay Hotel*). When three kids miss the last ferry to get off Raven Island during a school field trip and are stuck on the island overnight, they must outrun a killer, a weird ghost hunting crew, and a creepy flock of birds—and solve a generations-old mystery—if they want to survive until daybreak. Publication is set for summer 2022; Laurel Symonds at the Bent Agency negotiated the deal for world rights.

Subscribe to Publishers Weekly Children's (free) for a weekly roundup of book deals, so you can learn how to pitch your novel idea.

Writing the Jacket

Now that we have our short pitch, it's time to expand into plot. The best way to write a book jacket (or plot) description is to read A LOT of them. You get better at it, and you'll hone the pitch craft.

The good news: we can use this book jacket description for outlining, writing, editing, and pitching. A sharp pitch will reel you in when you are in danger of going off on a tangent when writing your novel.

Talk about value. Taking the time to create a strong book jacket description is worth the work.

A good book jacket is basically a sales pitch for your reader. You're inviting them to go on a 4 to 6 hour journey. Make it a good one.

This is what your plot description should tell your reader:

1. Who is solving the mystery? (your protagonist)
2. What's the mystery/crime?
3. Where are we going? (Setting)
4. When? (If this is a historical or futuristic novel.)

5. Why are we going? (the stakes for your protagonist, or the central conflict)

You can add comparable titles in the vein of, for instance: *readers of Stephen King's* IT *will enjoy this delightful clown horror story*.

Caution! One mistake I see writers make when they write this plot description is that they try to cram all the things into this text. Remember, it's a pitch. A good jacket gives you the broad strokes, the heart of the story, and entices you to want to buy it and read it. That's it.

You don't have to put everything in it. It's not an all-you-can-eat taco bar.

Your Turn

This may seem like a simple task, but it's not—you'll see when you try. Spend a week studying good book jackets, writing your own, and getting feedback from friends and family. Revise as needed.

Once more, with feeling: take the time to get this book jacket description right. It'll serve you throughout the entire novel writing, editing, and pitching process. It's the manual for your manuscript.

Chapter 3
Character

At this point, you probably have a good idea of what you want to write. You have your comparable titles picked and your novel's inspiration box (or office wall) created.

Now, you want to choose your main character—that protagonist you're about to send on a miserable quest. And there's a supporting cast of characters, of course.

Choosing a Protagonist

So, whose story should this be? There are entire writing craft books on character that will delve *deep* into this topic; if you feel you need the support, you can find them easily at your library or bookstore. But we're trying to move things along here.

Here's a good rule of thumb: your protagonist should be the person who is changed the most by your story's plot.

Whose story is this? Sometimes, we start writing from one perspective and find the story really belongs to someone else. Taking a minute to consider your protagonist will avoid you going down that particular rabbit hole. Take it from someone who's had to rewrite an entire novel because she picked the wrong protagonist: it's no fun.

That said, there's no one way to tell the story. Maybe you have multiple protagonists. Let's continue exploring this...

I Don't Want to Do This

Some years ago, I read this great book called *The Truth as Told by Mason Buttle* by Leslie Connor. I highly recommend it as a character study. Basically, Mason (the protagonist) doesn't want to remember how his best friend fell from the treehouse and died, even though Mason was there at the time. This book is more literary than mystery, but a great example of how to choose a protagonist.

An easy way to create character conflict is by choosing the person who *least* wants to be there as your protagonist.

This sounds complicated, but you basically build a character arc by having your protagonist overcome what makes them not want to go.

Here are more examples:

In *Midnight at the Barclay Hotel*, JJ just wants to go ghost hunting, not solve the mystery of Mr. Barclay's murder, especially since he's hiding a secret from his mom. Penny is afraid of *everything* but overcomes her fears by continuing her detective work with JJ and Emma.

In *Liar and Spy* by Rebecca Stead, Georges befriends a neighbor boy, investigates a mystery in his apartment building, and faces his grief and all the lies he tells himself. He would rather not join this investigation.

In *Daybreak on Raven Island*, Noah has severe anxiety. By facing his fears alongside his newfound friends, he is able to let go of some of his grief related to his mother's death and face the darkness (literally and figuratively).

I could go on for a while, but it's time to get to work now.

My Superpower Is...

Likewise, you want to think about what makes your character special. What's their superpower? In *Midnight at the Barclay Hotel*, Penny loves to read. This helps her solve the mystery surrounding Mr. Barclay; no one else has her superpower so that makes her special. In *Daybreak on Raven Island*, Marvin wants to make a scary movie. It's his desire to make his mark that drives a lot of his actions in the book.

Whenever I get stuck, I ask: what does my character want? How can I make getting this *so* hard that they must dive deep into their soul to get there? What makes them especially equipped to solve the mystery?

Supporting Cast

You can use a similar process to develop the supporting cast. I know, it's a lot of work, but then we *are* plotting a whole novel here...

Quick cheat: whenever I have trouble nailing down a character, I imagine which actor might play them if my book was a movie. Once I have a visual of what that character looks like, other traits fall into place.

Creating a mood board for your novel can be very helpful here. And no one has to know you based your antagonist on that actor you can't stand…

Quick cheat #2: If I'm still stuck, I start with a stereotype and build out. Take a successful CEO, for instance—she'd be very driven, right? But what happens when that CEO was once a homeschooling mom? You have JJ's mom in *Midnight at the Barclay Hotel*, a multi-dimensional character.

Pinterest, Canva, the walls in your office are all great places to make your characters come to life. Watch a few TV shows with a strong ensemble cast for inspiration (*The Bear*, *Big Bang Theory*, *Kim's Convenience*, *Schitt's Creek*, etc.), if you're feeling a bit lazy.

The Antagonist, or: the Suspects

The best mysteries have a three-dimensional antagonist, so you'll want to spend some time fleshing out this character. Who committed your crime, and why...?

Motive is the best way to develop your lineup of suspects as well. If you have your mystery to solve figured out, you'll just want to brainstorm one thing:

Who benefits from the crime?

This is pretty fun, and you'll likely expand your cast of characters. Each of your suspects can play the role of antagonist, since they won't want your detective to solve the mystery, lest their secret is outed. *Each* of your suspects can throw obstacles in the way of solving the mystery. You can have a lot of suspects, though be mindful that your cast doesn't overwhelm the reader. Too many new characters and it gets confusing.

While you're brainstorming suspects, think of ways they could fight back or hinder the investigation. It'll add conflict and mysterious elements as you plot.

Your Turn

Take one of your comparable titles (that's a published book like the one you're writing) and write up a similar condensed character analysis: X (character) overcomes Y (fear/reason they don't want to be there) by doing Z (external conflict/mystery/plot).

Once you get this, create a similar summary for your own novel-in-progress. It's okay if this feels crude and simple. You're just trying to get to the core of your character.

Chapter 4

The Crime

The Crime and Place

IN CASE YOU HADN'T noticed yet, I really love mysteries and crime fiction. As a reader, it's so much fun to put the clues together. The best mysteries also delve into why the antagonist might commit the crime—mysteries are really a study in psychology.

You wouldn't have picked up this book if you weren't also interested in mysteries on some level, so you probably know what I'm talking about. So how do you make your mystery a fun journey for your reader?

There are two approaches I have found effective.

First, you can start with the resolution, the solve to your mystery, and work your way backward.

Another approach is to write your way through it. For *Midnight at the Barclay Hotel*, I had no idea who of the four suspects actually killed Mr. Barclay. When writing my rough draft, I simple uncovered the killer along with my kid sleuths. I then went back and added clues during the revision process.

Think about *when* you want your reader to have certain clues. A good mystery is all about the timing of clue revelation. You want that treasure hunt to be a fair game.

Whatever the approach to writing your mystery, you should carefully pace your revelation. The last thing you want is for your reader to piece the solution together by page twenty.

Where to Find a Crime

The title of this section sounds wrong, but I get this question a lot: how do you pick the crime and corresponding mystery for your novel, especially if you're writing middle-grade? Some crimes are just too dark or gory—so how do you pick the right mystery?

For YA, you can delve deeper into the moral ambiguities of a crime, and you can even go fairly dark. YA horror has seen an uptick lately; sometimes those novels have a crime at the center of them that is so dark, mystery merges with horror. YA allows for crimes to explore the darker side of the human psyche that isn't really appropriate for kids.

MG is more akin to cozy mysteries; you can read on that side of genre if you want to see mysteries that lean away from darkness and are about the puzzle.

One easy place to look for an interesting mystery to feature in your book is history. Are there unsolved crimes in real life that you can play on in your mystery? For *Daybreak on Raven Island*, I used an unsolved Alcatraz prison escape as my mystery; I simply created my own fictional version of it and asked: what if those escapees made it off the island? How can I make that mystery relevant today? There must be a reason your kid/teen sleuth has to solve this mystery, or it won't create the sense of urgency and conflict you need to propel the story.

The benefit of linking your fictional story to a real-life one is that you have something to talk about during author visits. Also, if your crime is local to you, you now have local interest. My local paper did a nice write-up of me and my books because *Midnight at the Barclay Hotel* is set at a fictional version of the Stanley Hotel. The Stanley Hotel even sells my books!

If you do not have this kind of built-in opportunity, you can look at your novel's theme for direction. Is the story about parent relationships? Maybe that can be the whodunit of your mystery. Is your kid protagonist really into a sport, or some other activity? Maybe your mystery can be about athletic rivalry.

Take some time to brainstorm. Bounce ideas off your partner, kids, or critique partners.

Thriller vs. Mystery

Before *Midnight at the Barclay Hotel* was published, I wrote a spy adventure trilogy called Double Vision. Thrillers (or suspense novels) are mystery's big sister. They have a mystery at their heart, but the focus of the story is the chase. It's not whether the protagonist will solve the mystery, it's about *how* they're going to do it.

Thriller writing requires lots of pacing work; cliffhangers and action must be applied more carefully, along with clue revelation.

> **Thrillers are all about tension. Mysteries are all about the clue hunt and can move a little slower.**

Your Turn

What's the mystery your detective is going to solve…? Make sure it's age-appropriate for your reader.

You can look at the news if you are short on ideas, or check the internet for unsolved crimes…

Chapter 5
Setting and Research

By now, you may already have your setting picked out. Even if you do, consider your options, because setting can be such an important tool for writers.

An example: let's say you have a ten year-old protagonist who is having an argument with a parent. If you set the scene at the kitchen table, it'll be okay. But imagine this same scene at the movie theater (where you have to be quiet), on the soccer field (with the whole team watching), or on the side of the road, in the rain, while the car has a flat and the antagonist is on their heels...?

You can use setting to elevate the conflict in *every* scene.

Just give it a try and you'll see what I mean.

Research your setting with an eye for drama and you'll be well on your way to adding some (teen) spirit to your manuscript.

Research

By now, you should be eager to plot your novel already if you're anything like me. But sometimes, you feel like you just need to do a little more…

Research. Oh, how I love to get lost in reference books, the library (I bring two sturdy canvas bags to pick up my holds each week), or worse:

The Internet. (*cue horror music)

I love doing research, but I also know it's a big fat trap. Like going to the grocery store when you're hungry, or trying to find a movie to stream on Netflix on a Saturday night… You can lose about a bazillion hours not really getting much done at all.

Here's how you *don't* get lost in research, from someone who's been on both sides.

Ideally, you've done a good amount of research on setting and plot (and history—hello, fellow historical writers), so you shouldn't need to do a whole lot more. At this stage, too much research will stall your progress. We're here to write the book, not become a museum docent.

Here are a few questions to ask yourself about your novel project:

1. Do I have setting locked down?

I don't go into setting too much because my ideas often *start* with place, back in that fun brainstorming phase. At this point, I have a lot of research done already, at least to plot the novel. I hope you know *where* your story is happening.

2. Do I have my references clearly listed and handy, or in my idea box from chapter one...?

The problem with research is that as writers, we get lost in the story possibilities. If you just get going already, you can do targeted research as you write. Like: what do the roads look like in 1943 Amsterdam? Are there cobblestones? Details matter, but you can get really bogged down by them if you're not careful. It's how great novel ideas never get written. Keep a list of references handy, so you can quickly look up something if needed, but get back to writing.

3. Do I have a map?

I know, I bet you weren't expecting this. Aside from maps being cool, they also keep our plot progression in order. It takes a lot more work to fix a consistency problem when editing, like how long it takes to get from point A to B or how one would even get there, than it does to just have that figured out ahead of time.

Even if your setting isn't fictional, a map is really helpful. Get one or draw one.

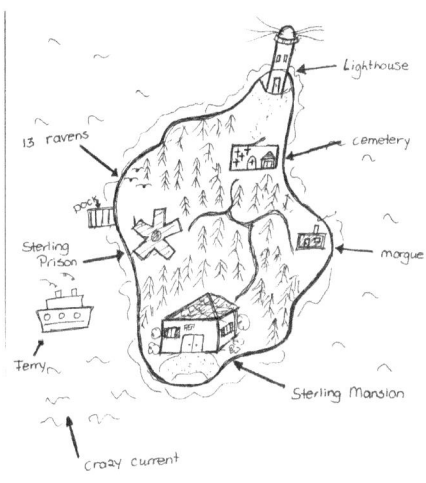

This is the original Raven Island map I drew for Daybreak on Raven Island, *my fifth novel for kids.*

You can use a timer as you research, or just a list of questions you're trying to answer before plotting. **The key is to have a time and task limit.** Once you get what you need, for the love of all that is holy, stop researching. Or you may never get to writing…

Tip from Fleur: if you need to look something up while writing, use a placeholder and come back to it later. That way you don't lose your writing momentum.

I use a few letter Xs as placeholders, like this: XXX. Easy to find just by scanning the text when I'm going back to edit.

Your Turn

Pick your setting and gather all your research. Ask yourself the three questions above, then move onto the next chapter.

Do not give in to the black hole of research…!

Chapter 6
Finding Time to Write

I'D LOVE TO BE *a writer, I just don't have the time.*

If you want to tick a writer off, you tell them that, I swear. I hear it anytime I tell people I'm a writer, from people I meet at a party to the Uber dude who drives me to the airport after I speak at a conference.

Honestly, it doesn't make me angry anymore, because I get it. It *is* hard to find time for something so lofty as to write a book, or any words at all. They say it takes 10,000 hours to master a craft. I've long surpassed that time, and I'm still learning—I'd argue that's the best part of being a writer in the first place. You're always the student, never the master.

Back to the issue of time. The thing is, none of us have unlimited time. It's all about deciding that it is important to you. Think of Future You: would (s)he like to say they've written a novel this year? I'll bet that would make the year great, right?

You can find the time if you really want to write. Here are some things I've done to get those books written.

Get Up Early

For my very first novel, I genuinely didn't have the time to write. I had two daughters who needed lots of time (I was homeschooling, long story), we were in the middle of a cross-state move (to Mississippi), staying in a temporary apartment because we'd just sold the house... My life was utter chaos.

And I had a dream book deal—three books, a MG spy series, with HarperCollins Children's. All I had was a partial manuscript written (this is not how books are usually sold, btw, but it's not important for this part). Only it meant I had to write a novel draft in 6 weeks. I had to find time.

So I got up at 5 AM to write, every day. It was rough, I'm not gonna lie. But there's something magical about being up before the rest of the world is. It's quiet, and you can focus. It also requires a good alarm clock, serious discipline and copious amounts of coffee.

I wrote and edited *Double Vision*, my first published novel, exactly that way. If you are trying to find time, getting up an hour early may be the best option for you. It's rough but worth it.

Steal Time

This 5 AM thing started to get harder when my evenings became busier and I got older. So for the second and third books in the Double Vision series, I started to steal time.

Basically, whenever I had a moment where I was waiting for a kiddo to take a gymnastics class, or they were busy with their schoolwork, I'd write. Twenty minutes here, twenty minutes there. I became good at hyper-focusing. It's a great exercise for any writer out there. I had no time for my inner critic to catch up, no time to doubt myself or overthink.

I just needed to write. Words on the page.

At the time, I averaged about 1,000 words a day. Some days, it was 250 words, some days more. But I had momentum, which can be the hardest to achieve.

Once you start rolling that boulder up the mountain, just don't stop...

If you don't believe you can steal your way to a finished novel, I give you *Double Vision: Code Name 711* and *Double Vision: The Alias Men*. These novels were written and edited entirely in stolen time.

If I can do it, you can, too.

As an aside: there's a whole thing called the Pomodoro method based on this time thieving approach. You can pop it your search engine if you want to learn more. I just like the idea of stealing time better.

Find Your Best Energy

Of course, both of these methods require discipline and won't work for everyone. But I challenge you to find an hour every day, if you want to FINISH a novel.

When's your best writing energy?

Think about when you produce the best writing, like when you just forget about time.

Are you a night owl or more of an afternoon writer? Are you an early bird, like me? Do you have a lunch hour during your day job hours...?

Figuring this out will help you tremendously. For instance, I'm not good any time after 3 PM, so I plan my day to have less creative activity during that time (like answering emails). My best writing energy is in the morning, so I protect that time from outside thievery, like laundry and other chore-type nonsense.

Your Turn

Pull out your planner, calendar or whatever you use to plan your schedule. When can you find time every day? Schedule it like you would a dental appointment with a cancellation fee.

Once you figure out how many words you can reasonably write a day, you can plan out how long it'll take to write that first draft.

Chapter 7
Plotting with Sequences

Why Sequences?

A HUNDRED YEARS AGO, movies were made on film that was rolled onto a reel. One reel could hold only ten, eleven minutes or so of footage before they needed to be changed out, so script writers had to put breaks in the story at these intervals. One sequence, ten minutes. In movies, you end up with roughly 8-10 sequences.

It's a story format that, as the consumers of story, we've gotten used to. Plus, for those of us who get a little overwhelmed when looking at a 300-page manuscript (that would be me), this sequence format helps to break the story up in neat chunks. One big manuscript is scary to write or edit. One sequence? More doable.

Note how I talk about using this method to edit as well. Sometimes, a story gets away from you. A character does something unexpected and you decided to run with it. Or you opted to figure out the story along the way, and now you have no idea what's even happening anymore.

Do not despair. This sequencing method can salvage your messy first draft or set up that shiny new idea that's been bouncing around your brain.

Optional: Prologue

If you want to get a good discussion going with lots of opposing views, ask the prologue-or-no-prologue question... Some people swear they skip over it, others say it should just be chapter one.

I like a prologue—as long as it's a good one. It bookends the story, can give a little backstory, tell the reader what kind of story they're about to read. In mysteries, a prologue sometimes gives an intriguing look at the crime that's at the heart of the story. These prologues can help hook your reader. In my case, more often than not, my books have a prologue.

Your story can have one too. Or not. The truth is that like everything else when it comes to writing, it's up to you. There are a few rules when it comes to prologues, however.

1. **Prologues need to have a certain disconnect from the story.** It can be that they cover a flashback, are written from a different character's perspective, or generally don't logically connect to the rest of the manuscript the same way. Still not sure? If the prologue could also be chapter one and flow logically into the rest of the book, it's not a prologue.

2. **Be cautious about using a prologue to overexplain the story in the beginning.** It's a good thing for readers not to know everything that happened. This way, they'll want to keep reading to find out more. Leave some mystery.

3. **Prologues shouldn't be so disconnected from the story that they feel tacked on.** If you're not sure, ask your critique group or beta reader(s) for feedback.

Final thought: you don't have to call it a prologue. Just stick it in front of your manuscript without a chapter number.

We can call it a bookend instead.

Sequence 1

This sequence is so fun to write. You can finally start telling this story that's been bouncing around your head and start following your character. It's the fresh beginning to your story.

It's also where writers drop the ball, which has big repercussions as one sequence stacks on the other.

Sequence one is the foundation to your manuscript. You want to make sure you set up everything that will make the rest sing.

This sequence is where we introduce character, conflict, setting, genre... Basically, we're following through on that spiffy book jacket description you wrote earlier. This sequence has a beginning, middle and end (with something of a cliffhanger, for fun).

By the end of Sequence 1, your character is being lured by the quest, but has decided it's not worth it (yet). Their character arc (remember that inner conflict they're trying to solve?) is keeping them from diving in, or at a minimum, they should be reluctant.

This part of your novel sets the tone, introduces character, conflict, setting, theme—it has to do a TON of heavy lifting. Make sure you have actual things happening.

We need conflict from the very beginning!

The biggest mistake writers make is that they start the story too soon (no inner conflict) or they rush toward the quest without setting up why we should care about the characters.

Let's look at this in action...

Examples

In Karen McManus's YA *You'll Be the Death of Me*, the story starts when the three teens go off in the car and drive on page 33 (hardcover edition). This book is a mystery version of *Ferris Bueller's Day Off*, so the call to adventure begins in a very obvious way. Much like going inside the closet in the *Chronicles of Narnia*, the characters are physically leaping.

In Rebecca Stead's MG *Liar and Spy* Georges has just moved into a new apartment and his dad encourages him to respond to an invitation on the bulletin board for a Spy Club. On page 16 (hardcover edition),

Georges grumbles about the whole thing—that reluctance of going on the quest.

Introducing the Mystery

Sequence one should give your reader a hint of the mystery to come. You want to introduce characters, conflict, and setting, but your mystery can still be somewhat in the background.

You don't have to introduce all your suspects just yet (that might get overwhelming), but a mystery is afoot! If you feel like you don't hint at the mystery enough, you can try a little foreshadowing. Something like, 'All is well, but everything is about to go sideways' is a good way to keep your reader curious to see what happens next.

Bottom Line:

Let's look at this simply, with a checklist. You want the following to happen in your first sequence:

1. Introduce your protagonist in their status quo environment. We should get an idea that things really should change, because...

2. We need conflict. This comes from your character arc: how is your protagonist going to change internally by the end of the book? Sequence 1 needs to set up the character in their current environment, before going on this journey.

3. Introduce the setting. Where are we, and how does this impact the story? Here, you have an opportunity to bring depth to the conflict.

4. Add a scene or moment where we see what makes your character special. What's their superpower? Readers need a way to identify with your protagonist and admire them, just a little. Is your protagonist kind, brave, strong, a good mother/son/spouse? Spend some time on this, especially if this is a series character.

5. Introduce at least some of your supporting cast. Remember, readers stick around for the characters. Plot is an easy fix, character arcs are much harder to create when it's time to edit.

6. What reason does your protagonist have to NOT want to go on this quest of yours? Really think about this, because you need inner conflict.

7. Outer conflict: who's your antagonist? How is the world going to make this journey difficult?

As you outline, try to work in scenes that have a beginning, middle and end that all work toward the end of sequence 1 plot point where your protagonist resists the call to adventure. Remember that character arc, the reason they don't want to go...? That's the end of this sequence.

Don't worry, we'll get to the quest in the next sequence. That's where the fun is after all.

Sequence 2

In sequence 1, we met your character in their status quo environment. The call to the quest is there, but your protagonist's inner struggle is keeping them from committing. Better to stay where you are than rock the boat, right?

Ha—*wrong*...

As the author, it's your job to rock the boat. Make your protagonist as uncomfortable as possible. Sequence 2 is all about cementing the conflict to be resolved. Your protagonist needs to be all-in (and in over their heads).

After denying the call to adventure in sequence 1, as the author, you now must build the case for going. With a beginning (perhaps, your protagonist contemplating this adventure), middle where pressure builds, to the end, where the kids go into the Narnia closet, etc.

Note: sometimes these two sequences are combined, to get a character off on the adventure quicker.

For you children's and MG book writers in particular, that may be the better plotting approach. We want to go on the adventure already... Just make really sure you've established your character motivation and arc, otherwise your reader won't be invested.

Examples

In Disney's *Up*, we meet Carl, the grumpy old man. We get his backstory in that brilliant short summary of his life with his wife, so we get who he is and why. There's the conflict of losing his house. Then there's the call to adventure.

We understand why he goes and creates that famous balloon house, right? But he first closes the door on that adventure, before deciding the only way out is up (see what I did there?).

In *Midnight at the Barclay Hotel*, the invitation to go to the Barclay Hotel for the weekend lures JJ to a weekend of ghost hunting. But he's also going with his mom, and he has a secret he needs to keep from her.... Conflict, built into the plot with character arc. By the end of the first sequence, everyone is at the Barclay Hotel. Because this is a book for kids, I combine sequence 1 and 2.

In *Daybreak on Raven Island*, the three kids are stranded on Raven Island for the night. Sometimes, the location literally forces your protagonist to go on whatever quest you want them to go on.

Minting Your Sleuth

Part of sequence 2 should involving minting your sleuth: you want your (amateur) detective to decide to take on the solving of your mystery. This can be very pronounced or more subtle, but the reader and your detective should know that we're about to do some sleuthing and clue collecting.

Bottom Line

For sequence 2, it helps to include the following:

1. A scene where your protagonist clearly states why they don't want to go, but feel they must. This can be inner monologue or a conversation with a supporting cast member.

2. Likewise, state why your antagonist does not want this quest to succeed. Again, this can be

interior monologue, a scene where the reader is privy to info that the protagonist is not, or some other situation where it's clear that there's an opposing force. If you're writing a mystery and don't want this to be too obvious (as in: you're trying to hide whodunit), you can hint at this opposing force. Just make sure it's clear that this quest is not going to be easy.

3. Find a moment to state your theme. You can use setting, an object, or be more direct and simply state it. Taking a beat to show your reader that there's deeper meaning to this story, and the quest will be worth it in the end.

4. Set up how your protagonist may 'win' the battle in act III/sequence 7 and 8. What makes them special? You already told us in sequence 1, now really bring it home so we believe it.

5. The final scene in this sequence has to show your protagonist actively decide to be all-in on this quest. You can isolate them using setting, but there should be a decision moment where your protagonist says *Let's go.*

Take the time to build your foundation in sequence one and two. The rest of your book will rest on it, so it should be solid.

Sequence 3

So we have a solid start to a book. A lot of the hard work is done, but then why is it that most novels go off the rails in the middle?

The hard part about outlining and writing the middle is that you can't force your way to the end of the story. You have to earn it.

There has to be a cause and effect to your plot, which is why there is no one-size-fits-all plot outline.

The good news is, you can use sequences to guide you.

Sequence 3 should build on what you've set up. Your characters are in the (new) world you've created. Your protagonist is trying to solve the conflict/problem you've created. They're making new friends, gaining new allies and knowledge (and clues!). You're already setting them up for the final battle in sequence 7.

But first, we have to earn the battle at the end.

Start this sequence by building your new world. Increase the conflict. By the end of sequence 3, your protagonist should think they have a good solution to the problem. It's not the right one, but it should make sense to your protagonist. Meanwhile, your antagonist is sputtering too. You'll want to hint at the 'battle' (whatever shape this will take) in the end.

See how vague this is? Frustrating, I know. It helps to know what genre you're writing to guide you.

In any romance (particularly on TV), we'll start seeing the protagonist flourish a little. Maybe there's a makeover…! I'm thinking of *Miss Congeniality* here.

If you're writing a literary novel, your character will be challenged and kicked out of their comfort zone.

In a fantasy novel, you start introducing the new world, the rules of that world, and the supporting cast. Try to have stuff happening while you do this, so you don't bore the reader.

Examples:

In *Midnight at the Barclay Hotel*, JJ, Penny, and Emma start investigating the motive of the suspects in Mr. Barclay's murder. This is a very straightforward approach to the third sequence, since this is a mystery. The challenge is to have the interviewing of suspects feel natural in the plot. After all, your detective is a kid or teen...

In Karen McManus's *You'll Be the Death of Me*, on page 78 of the hardcover, the three teens are trying to solve the mystery of a classmate's murder. When they see a mysterious person at the scene of the crime, they decide to follow him. That's a classic element of a mystery and corresponding investigation by an amateur sleuth.

Following a suspect or chasing down a lead is exactly the kind of story element to move a mystery along.

Your plot is like a shark: it has to relentlessly move forward, or it dies. Your reader will abandon your story (which we don't want, of course).

Think of using a plot point at the end of this sequence that you're working towards, like a stop on the road trip that is your novel.

Interviewing Your Suspects

For your kid or t(w)een sleuth, this sequence is all about collecting clues. Expect your list of clues to balloon, and you may even plan a scene where your detective takes stock. You know how on TV shows, the sleuth has a dry-erase board with pictures of suspects and clues written underneath them? This is that scene.

Giving your young reader a minute to catch up and follow along can be a plot point in itself. If your detective gains an ally, maybe they take a moment to explain the case. You don't need to reinvent the wheel here, just make sure you carve out a moment for the detective(s) to summarize the clues and go over what they've learned. Especially when you're writing MG, you'll want to guide your reader along, just a little.

Bottom Line

Here's a list of elements you'll want in this sequence:

1. Explain the rules of the new world. In science fiction and fantasy novels, this is pretty self-explanatory. In mysteries, you'll want to create a plan of attack when it comes to the investigation. How is your protagonist going to solve the crime? In literary novels, this sequence will be more about character change: your protagonist wants to solve the conflict and is trying new stuff to do so.

2. Introduce your supporting cast. Is there a mentor, a character who challenges your protagonist or who is an opposite? If you're writing a mystery, this is when you'll want to introduce the suspects.

3. Add a subplot. Using theme and your protagonist's character arc, add a subplot to your book. For example, if your protagonist is coming to terms with a bad relationship with a parent, you can echo this theme with a subplot that delves into a parental relationship.

Generally, this is a sequence where you build your plot and character arc. Allow for your story to gain momentum and complexity.

Sequence 4

As readers, we feel the storm coming. Your protagonist thinks they're going in the right direction with their conflict resolution, but they're wrong. (*insert evil writer laugh)

The important part about sequence 4 is that you're building tension and turning up the heat. Sequence 4 should build on sequence 3, which is why, again, there's no one-size-fits-all plotting system.

During sequence 4, we want to see your plot get more complicated, and for all of us to generally feel like stuff's about to hit the fan. Again, we want a beginning, middle, and end (with cliffhanger). You can either work towards a plot point or the midpoint of your novel.

Examples

In *Daybreak on Raven Island* on page 132 (hardcover edition), there is a new murder for the kids to solve. It's an easy way to escalate the plot or give the investigation a new direction.

The Clues Keep Coming

Sequence 4 is all about building on what your detective learned in sequence 3. It's important that what they do is a logical continuation of clues gathered before. For example, if there was a flower delivery at the crime scene, your sleuth will want to go to the flower shop to find out who delivered the flowers (and who ordered them). Bad mysteries often get this wrong: they shoehorn the character into a situation the writer decided they wanted their sleuth to get into. Good mysteries (and stories in general) go where the investigation would logically go.

Before deciding on plot events, make sure that the investigative logic tracks.

Checklist of sequence 4 elements:

1. Add an unexpected turn of events. Allow your protagonist to take a detour or segue.

2. Have your protagonist do something brave or out of character. We want to see them bust out of the mold we created in sequence 1, so we can earn that character transformation that we're working towards at the end of the book.

3. Don't forget to have your antagonist fight back. In mysteries, there should be a realization that this is a dangerous quest we're on. Make the stakes high.

4. Subplots should be getting more complex. Your protagonist is beginning to feel the heat.

5. Your protagonist is beginning to realize that the plan they came up with in sequence 3 may not work out. But they're still doggedly pursuing it the old way.

6. By the end of this sequence, you'll want a plot point that shows the complexity of the quest,

and that the protagonist may be in over their head.

Midpoint

The midpoint is exactly what the name implies: the middle of your book. This plot point is essentially a tentpole, holding your story up.

The midpoint is usually a reversal, a heightening of the stakes, or a redirect for your protagonist. If this sounds vague, it's a good thing: *you* can decide what direction you want your plot to take.

Examples

In thrillers this moment is often a heightening of the stakes. For example, in my spy-thriller for kids *Double Vision*, protagonist and spy-in-training Linc Baker realizes that the Mona Lisa with dangerous powers that he's trying to find isn't just dangerous to the city of Paris, it could hurt the whole world if it falls into the wrong hands.

Thrillers will sometimes introduce a time clock here. Only 24 hours until the bomb goes off…! You get the idea.

In mysteries, the midpoint is often a redirect in the investigation. Something is heightening the stakes (maybe our antagonist has killed before!), or changing the way your protagonist investigates the case.

Maybe your suspect isn't male, as the evidence suggested, but female. Maybe the investigation points to multiple suspects.

Maybe your protagonist becomes a suspect. This is an old trick, but it still works if you approach it in a fresh way.

In mysteries, the midpoint often brings a plot twist to the story.

Have some fun brainstorming how you could upset the applecart. There is a lot of possibility in the midpoint. You don't have to use all your ideas, but you may come up with a fresh twist that propels the next half of your novel.

If yours is a more character-driven story, you can use this part of the book as a turning point. Maybe your character does or thinks something that us readers would never expect them to do at the beginning of the book.

Look at this midpoint as the eye of the storm. Take a beat to sum up the investigation or have your protagonist do some reflection.

> **Note:** often, the reason writers struggle with the 'saggy middle' part of the story is because they haven't defined their midpoint.

Take the time and you'll thank yourself when you're writing the first draft and editing down the line.

Pivot Your Mystery

In a mystery, this redirect in the investigation often puts ALL the clues in new light. Maybe the timeline of events isn't what your detective thought, or their prime suspect has an alibi.

Have fun brainstorming this pivot. If you're not sure, read lots of mysteries (or cheat and watch TV) to see how other writers handled this.

Most importantly: have fun brainstorming. This plot pivot is one of the more important points in your story, so take your time to consider all the possibilities.

Midpoint possible scene list:

1. Have your protagonist take a moment to reassess and recalibrate. This is a good moment to summarize where we are.

2. Add a plot twist. What unexpected thing could happen here?

3. Add a timeclock and/or heightening of the stakes.

4. What could your protagonist do next that pushes their limits? Revisit your first sequence to look for ways your characters could behave out of character.

5. What is your antagonist doing? Imagine them having a moment here too, to recalibrate. If this was the antagonist's story, what would they do next that's pushing the limits?

6. Close this sequence with a new plan for your protagonist.

Sequence 5

So your detective has new clues, your thriller has heightened stakes, and/or your fantasy protagonist just realized this new world is not all it's cracked up to be.

Welcome to sequence 5. At this point, your protagonist should be shaking in their boots a little from the midpoint. Going on this quest is a lot harder than it looked, and they'd really like to go home now.

But we're past the halfway point, so it's full steam ahead. No going home for you, Dorothy.

How This Works in Practice

Sequence 5 should show your protagonist adjusting and making new plans. Your detective is pushing harder and digging deeper in their investigation. Your spy is pushing to the limit to stop the Horrible Thing from happening. In your fantasy novel, the new world becomes more hostile.

Your supporting cast may not be as nice as they seemed either. Your antagonist is definitely fighting back.

This is a good place to have a supporting character converse with your protagonist, to ask hard questions and hold up a mirror.

Do you have what it takes to complete this quest, Protagonist? Remember all those reasons you didn't want to go?

You'll want to solidify your protagonist's commitment to make it to the end. Their answer to these hard questions should be: *I'm in it to win it.* Even if they're scared. Sequence 5 is where we get back to slaying the dragon—or making plans to slay it anyway.

Sequence 5 is also where we'll start seeing your protagonist's character flaw come unraveled. If they're keeping a secret, it's about to come out...

Examples

In *Double Vision: Code Name 711*, our kid spy Linc just found out there's a double agent at work. BTW, this book has more twists and turns than a mountain pass. I loved writing it, but I definitely had to keep track of my notes...

In *You'll Be the Death of Me* on page 212 (hardcover), Ivy spills the beans on her involvement in an event that changed Mateo's life in the worst way. It's basically her fault that Mateo's family lost their business. Given that these two have a major thing for each other, this is bad.

Redirecting Your Mystery

In a mystery, the midpoint plot pivot will send your detective on a different path. Combined with their character arc, this sequence should feel like things are heating up and the clues are piling high.

Make sure you add a moment where your detective takes stock of the clues they have, even if they just do this solo or inside their head. Your reader needs a moment to catch up.

Sequence 5 Scene List:

1. A scene where the protagonist reaffirms their commitment to the quest.

2. A new plan for this second half, in response to the midpoint. If you're unsure, ask: what would my protagonist do, based on their character?

3. Gathering of the team. Your supporting cast is either joining in or bowing out.

4. Tackling of this new plan. Your antagonist should fight back.

5. A scene or two to tackle your subplot. Your protagonist should start feeling a little overwhelmed by all that's coming at them.

6. Result of this new plan.

Sequence 6

As you may have guessed, sequence 6 builds on sequence 5. All subplots come to a head and should resolve or be close to resolving by the end of this sequence. Your protagonist and antagonist are in a dance to lead them to the climax (sequence 7 and 8), but we're not there yet.

How This Works in Practice

This is a good place to thin your suspect list in a murder mystery and maybe have a red herring or two to challenge your protagonist. Your antagonist fights back. Friends may be bailing because this quest is just too hard. Maybe someone dies…? (Can you tell I'm a mystery writer or what?)

This sequence has a beginning, middle and end, leading to…

The End of Act II

Sometimes writers call this the darkness before dawn, but it doesn't have to be a dark night of the soul per se. That won't work for every novel.

Think of this point as the calm right before the storm.

Your protagonist realizes that the thing that made them not want to go on the quest in the first place is the thing they need to address. Maybe they're no longer afraid of the dark (or just found a metaphorical flashlight). Maybe they finally remember (this is a cheap but effective trick) the thing that's the key to the whole quest.

This is also a good spot to have a plot twist, for you fellow devious writers. You know, like the kind I have in *Midnight at the Barclay Hotel*...

Examples of Sequence 6

In *Liar and Spy* by Rebecca Stead, Safer's (and Georges's) imaginary world comes tumbling down. On page 147 (hardcover), their Spy Club and both their secrets are all exposed. This is a dark and difficult moment for both; this is a very character-driven mystery.

In *Midnight at the Barclay Hotel* in chapter 45, JJ's secret is out. Penny has just gone outside (in a blizzard) to find her grandpa, who had a run-in with the antagonist and is freezing to death outside. Penny has to be brave to save Grandpa.

Ruling Out a Suspect (or Two)

This sequence is where things come to a head, but also where, as a reader, the focus narrows. Eliminate a suspect. We should be down to two suspects by the end of the sequence, so we can start solving the mystery.

It's okay if your reader has figured it out; they'll stick around to see if they're right.

Sequence 6 Scene List:

1. Your protagonist takes a beat to sum up where they are. In a mystery, they summarize the clues, in a fantasy, we realize this world is not friendly, in a contemporary novel, your protagonist will feel like they're heading toward a cliff without the brakes on.

2. This is a good sequence for your protagonist to lose a friend or ally. Hit 'em where it hurts.

3. Have your antagonist fight back with the same determination as your protagonist. We should start anticipating the battle ahead. As readers, we should wonder whether our protagonist can win this.

4. Your suspect list should get smaller, with maybe two suspects left. This is often where mystery readers have solved the whodunit but stick around to see if they're right.

5. Toward the end of the sequence, wrap up your subplots. The end of Act II should act as a funnel for your plot, with upcoming Act III the focused end to your plot.

The end of act II can be a few scenes or a whole sequence.

Take a moment here, just like you did at the midpoint, to have your protagonist look at the world around them. Because in Act III, we're gonna solve that mystery. Maybe have your protagonist eat a snack and take a nap...

Sequence 7

It's time to solve the mystery, slay the dragon, (fill in your metaphor)…! Your hero has conquered their fears, gained and lost allies, and probably survived a plot twist or two. Phew!

But first: sequence 7. Because no one goes into battle without their armor.

This is where we prepare for whatever showdown you have planned for sequence 8.

Your protagonist gathers their (new) tools and comes up with a genius plan to defeat the antagonist in sequence 8.

So what does this mean if you're not *actually* storming a castle and your battle is more a metaphorical one? For mysteries, the investigation should come to a close. Even if your protagonist isn't a hundred percent sure whodunit, the reader should be able to put it together. We like to feel smart, us bookish folk.

In a heist, your protagonist is pulling out a map of the place they're about to rob. They've gathered their motley crew to complete the job.

Using Setting

Try bringing your protagonist back to (one of) the opening settings. It makes the whole book feel deeper and shows how far your protagonist has come in their character arc.

Solving the Mystery

Remember the dry-erase board in sequence 3? All those clues your detective gathered? Everything should come to a head here, where only one suspect could have done it. There can be NO DOUBT. If you need to tie up some loose ends, confirm an alibi, or identify a red herring, this is the place to do it.

Your detective solves the mystery. Your reader goes, 'But of course!' Everyone feels smug and smart.

Scene List for Sequence 7:

1. Your protagonist's character arc should be coming to a close. A scene where readers see your new and improved protagonist in action will add depth to your novel.

2. It's time to gather the team for our plan to storm the castle. Even if you're not literally storming the castle or slaying a dragon, your protagonist will be working toward doing Something Big. Doing this with a team is always better.

3. Anything you didn't wrap up in sequence 6 should be addressed here. Create whatever scenes you need to do so.

4. Your antagonist is also planning to win the battle in sequence 8. Make sure you at least hint that it won't be easy.

5. How is your protagonist thinking they'll win the battle? Is there a flaw we as readers (and perhaps a supporting cast member) see in this plan?

Sequence 8

The showdown! That's literally what I call this sequence in my plotting. Whatever you've been plotting towards, this sequence is it. I won't go on too much about this part of the novel, because it should be very straightforward. Oftentimes, this is the easiest part to write. But...

Consider heightening the stakes even more. How could this moment be more dramatic? How could the character arc/transformation feel more significant?

Challenge yourself as a writer as you plot this sequence. It can take a story from good to great.

Examples

In *Daybreak on Raven Island* on page 210, the three protagonists confront the antagonist in the island's graveyard, using their movie-making skills to draw the killer out.

In *The Truth as Told by Mason Buttle* on page 265, Mason is finally coming to terms with what happened when his best friend fell from their treehouse and died. He is ready to take his diary that explains events to the detective who has been pressuring him to remember.

Wrapping Up Your Mystery Without a Bow

The mystery is solved, justice is served, and we can all go home. Word of caution: don't wrap everything up in a bow, or your mystery will choke. Life is rarely so easily solved, so leave some ambiguity. Just not too much if you're writing a MG…

This sequence ending is a good spot to drive home theme(s) that you identified in your plot. It'll make your mystery feel like it matters.

Scenes for Sequence 8:

1. The mystery is solved, and now we see the aftermath. What happens to all the characters?

2. The mystery has the smallest twist at the end. Maybe a clever clue you placed early on now comes to light. Did the antagonist have an accomplice, perhaps? Or did your detective have a mysterious friend who helped without them realizing it? Is a missing person/pet suddenly found? This is a good spot to have some fun.

3. Is your book part of a series? You'll want a cliffhanger at the end, to hint at the mystery to come in book 2.

Chapter 8
Placing Clues and Red Herrings

THE QUESTION I GET most often from fellow writers is: where do I put the clues in my mystery? Just like the outline, there's unfortunately no one-size-fits-all approach. Clue revelation is something you'll do more by instinct—once you've read a whole lot of mysteries.

There are a few tricks, however, to help you along.

1. **Outline your detective's investigation ahead of time.**

How is your detective going to solve the mystery? You can use the solution and work backwards, or just start at the beginning, but you'll want to have at least a rough idea of how your sleuth will get to the big revelation at the end. Even if you're more of a fly-by-the-seat-of-your-pants writer, outlining the investigation will help make your mystery solid. Think of the clues as breadcrumbs your sleuth follows to get to grandma's house.

2. Keep it logical.

The reason there's no one solution to clue placement is that one clue should lead to the next. You want your investigation to be logical. Think about it from your kid detective's perspective: what would they do next?

3. Place your (real or false) clues at the end of a sequence.

Ideally, your sleuth finds out something new in each sequence, so you can simply place a clue or two at the end of each one. Again, think of this as the next logical breadcrumb you want your sleuth to find.

4. Surround your clues with red herrings.

Worried you're being too obvious? You can surround your clues with false ones—information that your sleuth thinks is relevant, but we find out is just a tangent or irrelevant information. By the end of your story, your detective should be able to identify those false clues (called red herrings in the mystery world). You can even have them go off on an investigative tangent, just don't let that go too far and for too long in a bad direction.

5. Always play fair with your reader.

There is nothing that irks me more than a mystery where, as a reader, I couldn't have solved the mystery along with the sleuth, or where there's a giant clue dump at the end. Play fair with your reader. Mysteries are a puzzle to solve—the fun comes from feeling smart enough to put the clues together. It's a game of wits where everyone wins, writer and reader alike. Well, your antagonist doesn't win, of course...

The Double Plot Twist

Plot twists are fun, and the mystery genre definitely allows for some good ones. Another approach to writing your ending can be to have a double twist. Thrillers like to do this sort of thing; it takes careful plotting but can be a fun game of cat and mouse with your reader.

Basically, your protagonist thinks they are done solving the case, everyone is high-fiving, but there is that sneaky feeling that there's a loose end… Maybe your sleuth solved the case, but there is a grander guilty party/force still to be revealed. Maybe there's more than one culprit, and the second one got away. In *Double Vision: The Alias Men*, our spy kid Linc Baker caught the culprit, but he finds out that there's an overlord-type force at play.

This double-twist section is also a good place to set up a series. With a cliffhanger, readers will know that there's a to-be-continued part of the story.

What to Do If You Get Stuck

You're knee-deep in your mystery, you're happily writing along, but then there's that sneaking suspicion that your story is kinda... Boring. Sure, the characters are having their moment, you're explaining the new world, but it doesn't feel high stakes.

Here are a few solutions to low tension:

- Someone is following your protagonist.

- There's a mysterious package, envelope, phone call, email.

- There's a car or bicycle chase.

- Introduce a deadline: if the mystery isn't solved by this time, the consequences are dire.

All of these are false clues or diversions from your mystery, but they can add questions that ratchet up the tension.

Some Tips from Fleur

Just as you thought you were done, here are a few ways you can revise the whole outline, now that you've made it to the end:

1. Use the sequences to place clues, real or false. You can work toward a plot revelation with each one, to make your pacing strong.

2. Use this same method to gradually change your protagonist. How can they s*looowwwlly* change throughout the book, with one step building on the previous one?

3. Don't forget about your villain! Antagonists fight back, or the story is dull and flat. Try revealing more of your antagonist's motivation and thinking to the reader, so they can see how stuff will go wrong in Sequence 8.

4. What's your theme? Use this to develop any subplot, supporting cast's journey, even small things like what book your protagonist is reading or movie they're watching. It will add depth to your story.

5. More fun ways to play with theme: try adding an object or person that reflects the theme. In

the movie *Up*, we remember those balloons and the house they carry, right? I'll give you a split second to think about all the thematic significance. Those Pixar people know what they're doing...

Your Turn

Plot your novel. You got this.

Chapter 9
Rough Draft and How to Stay Motivated

CAN YOU BELIEVE THAT all we've done so far is outline your novel...? As you can tell, I'm a big believer in planning, especially when it comes to writing a novel. It's very easy to get overwhelmed by the sheer size of the endeavor. The outline will help you stay on task, break down the work into manageable chunks, and it will guide you when it's time to revise.

More on that later.

Right now, it's just time to write the first draft. It's the most terrifying, exhilarating part of writing. And it's a confidence game between you and your inner critic.

How to Stay Motivated

It never fails: I get 10K words into a first draft and I start to lose steam. What if this novel is a bad idea? What if I stink as a writer?

Maybe I should just quit and call it good. Focus on a different idea. Maybe I'll write a picture book – those are easy, right?

(They're actually harder. Try to write one sometime and you'll see.)

Staying motivated is about outrunning your inner critic.

I find that my inner critic doesn't wake up until about nine in the morning, so I write in the early hours. This also works for those of you juggling a day job or family while writing (hats off to you, writer friend).

Sometimes you need to remind yourself of why you were writing this book in the first place. Imagine that kid reader, feeling seen and getting lost in your book. There's nothing like it, let me tell you.

I hang kid art over my desk to remind me of my end game, and who is my boss. Not the publishing industry, not the parents or even the teachers are who I write for. I write for the kids. That art is what I need to see every day to keep my eye on the ball.

Find out what motivates you and remind yourself when you run out of steam.

The Art of the Rough Draft

If you looked at any famous writer's first draft, you'd probably find a pretty rough manuscript. Personally, I've come to accept that this is what the process looks like. But when you haven't written a lot of novels, the roughness of your first draft may be discouraging.

Here's the truth. First drafts, quite frankly, are supposed to be bad. Revision is where we'll clean it all up. For now, you just want words on the page. In fact, let that be your mantra.

Words on the page. You need a rough draft to have something to edit.

Using Placeholders

Keep your momentum going by using placeholders. My rough drafts are riddled with XXXX which is what I use when I forgot a character's name or the street or whatever. I also add notes to myself in ALL CAPS, like when I think there's an opportunity for a cool metaphor or I just need to research something.

Placeholders are your friend.

Taking Notes

Remember that notebook (or file) you used to brainstorm and outline your novel? Use it to take notes while writing. Found something you need to research? Jot it down.

Once this rough draft is done and you've taken a moment to catch your breath, your notes will be handy to focus your revision. For now, we just want to keep on swimming, like Dory from *Finding Nemo*.

Words on the page.

Your Turn

Define what motivates you to write. It can be more than one thing—in fact, having multiple motivators may help you make it across the finish line faster. Write those down and put them somewhere you'll see it every time you write.

We all need fuel to keep the engine running. Find yours.

Chapter 10
Revision: Where the Real Work Happens

Y<small>OU FINISHED YOUR FIRST</small> draft! Woohoo! I would say this calls for cake...

Whatever your preferred form of celebration is, I hope you do. Writing a novel rough draft is a big deal, and you should celebrate your accomplishment.

The Importance of Taking a Break

Your excitement over this finished draft may cause you to feel like you're ready to start revising this thing right away. I'm here to give you some advice.

Don't do it.

Taking a break allows the dust to settle, for ideas to float to the surface of your consciousness, and for you to generally refill the creative well. Take a day off and do something fun. You deserve it. Let that manuscript cool, at least for a few weeks.

Keep your notebook handy, because stuff will pop into your brain while you're doing other things. Maybe you'll see some connection, a deepening of character or theme. Or maybe you just remembered your timeline isn't entirely correct.

Whatever it is, it'll wait.

Taking a solid break gives you the perspective you need to revise.

Revision Strategies

You may find once you go back to your manuscript that it's a hot mess. Or maybe you'll see those moments of brilliance, when the writing was flowing, and you could see the story play out. Most likely, it'll be a combination of things.

1. Print out your manuscript

Even if you feel it's a waste of paper. Plant a tree for this step, but do it. Getting a visual, tactile impression of your manuscript is so valuable. First off, it shows you all your hard work (yay You!). Also, it'll make it easier to split the revision into manageable chunks.

2. Split by Sequence

Next, find yourself eight or so manuscript clips, and clip each sequence together. Are any sequences shorter than others? That may mean you have to flesh out some chapters. Do you have a very long sequence? Maybe you need to trim, or split it into two. We'll figure that out later. For now, just breaking up all these pages into plot-focused sections will help.

3. Read it

Set aside a week or whatever time you need to read the whole thing. Resist the urge to copyedit or proofread—we're just reading for the big picture changes. Where does the plot feel rushed? Where do big plot moments just don't seem that big? Read with a bit of distance, as if the manuscript belongs to someone else. If this were your critique partner's project and they asked you to give feedback, what notes would you give?

4. Note Big Changes

For each sequence, reference your plot outline and note parts that are different (that's normal). Sometimes the coolest stuff doesn't come together until you let your characters loose and allow them do what they're gonna do.

Does each sequence have a beginning, middle, and end? Does each sequence build logically onto the previous one?

Do the characters live up to the cool character arcs you built during the plotting phase?

Do the clues feel logical? Does your resolution come as a result of your kid sleuth solving the mystery? We don't want random events to fall into their lap. Make your sleuth work for the final aha! moment.

5. Create a Revision List

Now, with all these notes from your readthrough, create a revision list. What big changes do you need to make to fix the problems you've identified? Big changes only, to start. We'll get the small stuff later.

I create a checklist—of scenes to add, revise, heighten in tone, or flesh out. That way, I can check each item off as I complete it.

6. Revise

With your revision list, make a rough estimate of how long you think it'll take to complete ALL OF IT. This can feel overwhelming when you're revising a novel-length manuscript for the first time, and that's normal. This first round of revisions is HARD. But once you find an agent and your editor sends you an editorial letter, this is exactly what you'll have to do to get that revision done. It's important to know that you can analyze your own work, identify high-level, big picture problems, come up with a plan to address these, and know how long it'll take to finish the work.

Pull out your calendar. Decide when you will revise. And do the work.

Round Two, Three, Four.

Not to depress you or anything, but you'll probably have to go through this revision process a few more times. But once you have a system (and you should come up with your own that works for you), this is just another day at the office (or writing desk).

Writing is rewriting and then rewriting a dozen times more. You'll know you're getting somewhere when you're sick of looking at your manuscript.

Copyedits

Clean up the typos, the inconsistencies, the times you repeat yourself. You can do this on paper or on the computer. And consider changing the font so your eyes pick up on things they didn't before.

Done!

This calls for cake again, I say. Celebrate with that family you've been ignoring while you wrote. Celebrate with your writing buddies.

You did it. This is a big deal. Make it feel like one.

Chapter 11
Marketing & Selling

First: congrats again for finishing your MG or YA mystery! Hopefully, you've had your cake or other celebratory moment and are now wondering how to get this amazing book into the hands of young readers.

The Kidlit market is a little different than the one for adults. Pull up a chair, pop a squat, criss-cross-applesauce, and I'll explain.

Getting Past the Gatekeepers

The peculiar thing about marketing books for kids is that the people who are buying the books will often never read it. We call those folks the gatekeepers, which makes them sound ominous when they're not. Really, they're just teachers, librarians, parents, and other adults who buy the book for your kid or teen reader.

In Kidlit, the people who buy the book may not be your reader.

A Note on YA Readers

This rule does not apply to YA, of course, because YA likes to make its own rules, like the surly teen it is. There are no gatekeepers typically, unless you have a middle school kid who is browsing the school library.

You can write what you want in YA.

An important statistic, however, is that a lot of YA readers are not even teens. And when I say a lot, I mean, like, *a lot*. The research isn't exact (the buyer vs. reader discussion again), but let's say at least half of YA readers are adults. Not that this really matters a whole lot when it comes to the actual writing, but it's something to consider and the sales side.

Still. Write the YA mystery you want and let your publisher figure out what the marketing plan is going to be. Now, about that...

Agents, Editors, and Small Presses

If you are new to traditional publishing, welcome! This industry is topsy-turvy sometimes, so let me give you a quick lay of the land.

If you want to be published by any of the Big 5 – that's Hachette, HarperCollins, Macmillan, Penguin Random House, Simon and Schuster and their numerous imprints, you need an agent to submit to editors. Editors simply don't have time to weed through thousands of manuscripts a month (yup, it's crowded out there!), so they count on agents to filter out the good stuff.

You are the good stuff.

You'll need an agent if you want to crack this segment of the market. Plus, agents can represent you when it's time to sign contracts, get you more money, and generally be your advocate in business.

Where to Find Kidlit Agents

Of course, you don't just want any agent, you want one who knows their way around children's, middle-grade, and/or YA, depending on what kind of mystery you wrote. Ideally, that agent also likes mysteries.

That's a pretty darn specific kind of agent. They do exist, however.

Here are some places you can research agents to query:
AgentQuery
Publishers Marketplace
ManuscriptWishlist

Query Letters, Synopses, Formatting

There are ample examples of query letters online, though everyone has varying opinions on what this should look like. I could fill a whole book with submission strategies and such, but I'll keep it short here. There isn't anything you can't find on the internet these days.

When in doubt, keep it simple. Use the short pitch as your query opener, and the book jacket description as your query letter body (see how all that hard work we did in the first few chapters pays off now?). Remember that if you are pitching an agent or editor, you're asking them to partner in producing a book. It's a business decision for all parties whether to join forces or not, so behave professionally when the rejections start coming in. Book publishing is a small world; people will remember if you do something unprofessional.

Small Press

Maybe you can't get an agent to take the bait. Maybe you just don't feel like going through the pain and time wasted on the query process (it can be long and tedious for sure). There are small presses who publish children's and/or YA mysteries, and you can query them directly. You are tossing your query in what's called the slush pile, just to be warned. It's called a slush pile, because... Well, use your imagination. It's a numbers game, but it's not impossible.

Independent or Self-Publishing

Once upon a time not that long ago, I would've advised against independent or self-publishing a MG or

YA book. It's very hard to get books into schools and libraries when you don't have the backing and distribution channels of a publishing house to get you there. Never mind getting the trade reviews…

It's still hard to do this on your own, but there are people who've been successful. Study them. What did they do to be successful? Can you follow suit? I'm a big believer in not reinventing the wheel. If there's an author out there you admire, follow them. Without being a creepy troll, of course. You're too cool for that.

The Kidlit and Mystery Community

We all need friends to get ahead in this bananas publishing business, and I highly recommend you find your people. Without a few amplifiers of your signal (and generally, friends to have coffee with), you simply won't succeed.

On the children's writer and illustrator side, you'll want to start by joining SCBWI. Yes, it costs, but you'll get your annual membership back in spades when it comes to resources and support, both on the published and pre-published side. There is a national organization, but you'll probably get the biggest benefits from joining your local chapter events. Some of my best friends and strongest supporters I met through SCBWI. I can't recommend it enough.

Mystery Writers Organizations

On the mystery side, you have some options.

International Thriller Writers (ITW) doesn't cost to join and may be an all-round benefit if you write thrillers. They have an annual conference in New York City, but no local chapters. They have a nice support system for debut authors.

Mystery Writers of America (MWA) is the most established of the bunch. They have a national chapter and local chapters, though your mileage may vary depending on where you live. They have an annual Edgar Award for Juvenile and one for YA, which is one of the few organizations that has a younger age award category for mystery. My local chapter is great, so I get a lot of benefit from networking and their educational programming. Check yours out and consider joining to get an idea of how they might help you.

Sisters in Crime (SinC) came about because women generally get the short end of the stick (you can look up the history), especially in the mystery genre. You don't have to be a woman to join, and the networking benefits can be great all the way around. As with MWA, there's a national chapter and local chapters with events and programming. It's been well worth it for me, though again your mileage may vary depending on where you live.

That covers it for the bigger organizations. You may have local ones; I also recommend checking out your nearest independent bookstore, to see if there are any events of interest for writers.

Get to know your local bookseller. They'll be your best friend when it's time to sell your book...

Chapter 12
School Visits and Speaking

ALTHOUGH IT CAN BE tough to sell children's books, there are some benefits to writing for kids. One of the biggest: you can do school visits. But you will have to be comfortable being a speaker (and talking to kids) for this to work.

It's okay if you don't. I have many author friends who don't do school visits, either because they have a day job that prevents them from it, or because they just don't want to. Every author is different.

There are several benefits to school visits.

For one, you can talk directly to your kid reader. You can find out what they're into (my favorite thing), and you can feel uplifted by adoring kid fans. Author school visits never fail to feed my soul.

If you are wondering if you can charge for these presentations, the answer is yes. There are many authors who do school visits for free, though my experience has been that if you work for free people treat you like you're worth nothing. That said, I certainly don't judge an author or illustrator who doesn't charge for their talks. Sometimes it's the only way to get your book out there.

Many full-time authors make a good chunk of their living from school visits, library talks, and (writer or literacy) conference talks.

I could write a whole 'nother book on this writing-as-a-business topic… Do your own research to see if this is a goal for you.

What do you even talk about? I do a fun talk on plotting a mystery. You can talk about anything related to your book. If you're struggling, ask your critique partners to brainstorm with you—it's fun, and friends often have a better view of what unique perspective you bring to the table. Anything educational is a plus.

What research did you do for this book you're writing? That's always a good topic to start with.

Chapter 13
Final Thoughts and Resources

Hopefully, you've found this book helpful to write your mystery for kids. Wanna know a secret...?

You can use this blueprint to write *any* book. Mystery, kidlit—it all comes down to simply a good story where there's a (mystery) plot and the characters are interesting. That's it.

I hope you are successful in your writing career.

And drop me a line, will ya? It gets lonely out here in the writing room.

Say hi! I can always use another friend in mystery.

Find me online: www.fleurbradley.com

Books

Brody, Jessica. (2023), *Save the Cat! Writes a Young Adult Novel*. Ten Speed Press.

Ephron, Hallie. (2017), *Writing and Selling Your Mystery Novel*. Writer's Digest Books.

Klein, Cheryl. (2016), *The Magic Words: Writing Great Books for Children and Young Adults*. W.W. Norton & Company.

Liu, Cynthea. (2023) *Writing for Children and Teens: A Crash Course*. Pivotal Press.

Mystery Writers of America. (2022), *How to Write a Mystery*. Scribner.

Tharp, Twyla. (2006), *The Creative Habit: Learn It and Use It for Life.* Simon & Schuster.

Websites

Agentquery: agentquery.com

International Thriller Writers (ITW): itw.org

Mystery Writers of America (MWA): mysterywriters.org

Manuscript Wish List: manuscriptwishlist.com

Publishers Marketplace: publishersmarketplace.com

Publisher's Weekly: publishersweekly.com

Sister in Crime (SinC): sistersincrime.org

Society of Children's Book Writers and Illustrators (SCBWI): scbwi.org

About Fleur Bradley

Fleur Bradley writes short crime fiction and novel-length mysteries for kids, including award-winning *Daybreak on Raven Island* and *Midnight at the Barclay Hotel* (Viking/PRH), and the Double Vision trilogy (HarperCollins). Recently, she compiled her process for writing mysteries for t(w)eens in *Get a Clue: How to Plot, Write, and Sell Your MG or YA Mystery*.

Fleur is a literacy advocate and speaks at educator conventions on reaching reluctant readers. She lives in a cottage in the foothills of the Colorado Rockies where she likes to foster rescue animals.

Find Fleur online at fleurbradley.com.

Fleur Bradley's Books

Daybreak on Raven Island (Viking/ Penguin Random House)

TLA Bluebonnet Award List
Agatha Award nominee
Anthony Award nominee
Winner of the Colorado Authors League Book Award for Best Juvenile/YA
Battle of the Books favorite

From the critically acclaimed author of *Midnight at the Barclay Hotel* comes a thrilling new middle grade mystery novel inspired by Alcatraz Prison.

Tori, Marvin, and Noah would rather be anywhere else than on the seventh grade class field trip to Raven

Island prison. Tori would rather be on the soccer field, but her bad grades have benched her until further notice; Marvin would rather be at the first day of a film festival with his best friend, Kevin; and Noah isn't looking forward to having to make small talk with his classmates at this new school.

But when the three of them stumble upon a dead body in the woods, miss the last ferry back home, and then have to spend the night on Raven Island, they find that they need each other now more than ever. They must work together to uncover a killer, outrun a motley ghost-hunting crew, and expose the age-old secrets of the island all before daybreak.

Midnight at the Barclay Hotel (Viking/ Penguin Random House)

Winner of the 2021 Colorado Book Awards for Juvenile Fiction
Winner of FLA's Sunshine State Young Readers Award
A 2020 Agatha Awards Finalist
A 2021 Reading the West Book Award Finalist
A 2021 Anthony Awards Finalist

Featured on NPR's "Best of 2020" Middle Grade list

Hunting ghosts and solving the case before checkout? All in a weekend's work.

Read the novel that *New York Times* bestselling author, Chris Grabenstein calls, "My kind of mystery!"

When JJ Jacobson convinced his mom to accept a surprise invitation to an all-expenses-paid weekend getaway at the illustrious Barclay Hotel, he never imagined that he'd find himself in the midst of a murder mystery. He thought he was in for a run-of-the-mill weekend ghost hunting at the most haunted spot in town, but when he arrives at the Barclay Hotel and his mother is blamed for the hotel owner's death, he realizes his weekend is going to be anything but ordinary.

Now, with the help of his new friends, Penny and Emma, JJ has to track down a killer, clear his mother's name, and maybe even meet a ghost or two along the way.

Double Vision Trilogy (HarperCollins)

Spy Kids **meets** ***Diary of a Wimpy Kid*** **in F.T. Bradley's Double Vision trilogy.**

Follow Linc Baker as he takes the place of super kid spy Ben, taking him to Paris, Washington D.C, and Los Angeles. Only Linc has no idea how to be a spy... Will his antics and ingenuity save the day...?

Get the latest on Fleur Bradley's books and appearances on her website:

www.ingramcontent.com/pod-product-compliance
Lightning Source LLC
LaVergne TN
LVHW010343070526
838199LV00065B/5781